Henry Goodricke

Observations on Dr. Price's Theory

And principles of civil liberty and government, preceded by a letter to a
friend, on the pretensions of the American colonies

Henry Goodricke

Observations on Dr. Price's Theory
And principles of civil liberty and government, preceded by a letter to a friend, on the pretensions of the American colonies

ISBN/EAN: 9783337724849

Printed in Europe, USA, Canada, Australia, Japan

Cover: Foto ©Suzi / pixelio.de

More available books at **www.hansebooks.com**

OBSERVATIONS

ON

D.ᴿ PRICE's

THEORY and PRINCIPLES

OF

CIVIL LIBERTY and GOVERNMENT,

PRECEDED BY

A LETTER to a FRIEND,

ON THE

Pretenfions of the AMERICAN COLONIES,

In refpect of

RIGHT and EQUITY.

Diffentientium inter fe reprehenfiones non funt vituperan-
dæ: maledicta, contumeliæ, tum iracundiæ, contentiones,
concertationefque in difputando pertinaces, indignæ mihi
philofophia videri folent: - - - - - - - neque enim difputari fine reprehenfione, nec cum iracundia aut pertinacia
recte difputari poteft. CICERO *de fin. Bon. & Malorum.*
Lib. i. 8.

YORK:

Printed by A. WARD, for J. DODSLEY, T. CADELL, and
R. BALDWIN, London; and J. TODD, in Stonegate.
York. 1776.

ADVERTISEMENT

OF THE

EDITOR.

I Have not scrupled to make use of the permission
to publish these Observations on Doctor PRICE's
Theory and Principles, *together with the* Letter
*that precedes them. The Doctor and others have
been particularly confident in appealing to these principles as uncontrovertibly founded on Reason, and
supported by the best Authorities. With these confident pretensions the* Observations *of my friend seem
worthy to be contrasted; and as the Doctor particularly objects to nameless antagonists, I have prevail-d
on him to suffer his name to appear at the end of
the* Letter.

Any attempts to reconcile perfect Liberty *with*
Government *must ever fail, as they always have
done hitherto, either in theory or practice; and to
set up public pretensions to it is unhappily deluding
the unwary and undiscerning part of the people, and
sowing the seeds of unreasonable discontent. Doctor*
PRICE's *system seems reducible into as little compass*

as

ADVERTISEMENT.

as that, within which Mr. LOCKE *comprizes the scheme of Sir* ROBERT FILMER's Patriarcha,—— *only just in the other extreme.* FILMER's; That all Government is abſolute Monarchy, *and the ground he builds on is this,* That no man is born free. *Doctor* PRICE's; That all Government is or ought to be a Democracy, *and the foundation of his ſyſtem is this,* That ſelf-government is unalienable. *Between theſe two are ſeveral mediums, which Reaſon and Experience recommend, and which have the ſanction of Mr.* LOCKE *and of the moſt eſteemed writers on Civil Government.*

Many anſwers have been publiſhed to Doctor PRICE's *pamphlet, but none, it is preſumed, that ſuperſede the utility of this; the ſpecial intent and object of which are ſufficiently explained by the writer himſelf. The haſte, with which things of this temporary nature are written and publiſhed, may poſſibly have left ſome ſmall inaccuracies of ſtyle and expreſſion; for which the critical and candid reader will make due allowance. One error of the preſs, as being a very material one, I muſt mention here; it occurs page 44 in the note, line 14, where for* reſiſtible *read* irreſiſtible.

June 20, 1776.

CONTENTS.

SECT.

CONTENTS.

ERRATA.

Page 23.   line 9.   For *particularcir cumflances* read *particular circumflances*

27.   l. 14.   For *principle* read *principles.*

44. note l. 14.   For *refiflible* read *irrefiflible.*

61.   For *gouvernmens* read *gouvernemens.*

For *Liv.* x. read *Liv.* xi.

112. l. 26.   For *refolutions* read *revolutions.*

113. l. 1.   For *refling* read *vefling.*

LETTER

TO A

FRIEND,

ON THE

Pretensions of the AMERICAN COLONIES,

In respect of

RIGHT and EQUITY.

A

L E T T E R

T O A

F R I E N D,

On the Pretenfions of the AMERICAN
COLONIES, in refpect of

R I G H T and E Q U I T Y.

DEAR SIR!

I Herewith fend you my *Obfervations* on
Doctor PRICE's Principles of Government
and Civil Liberty. If they appear to you
juft and important, you are welcome to make
them public, together with this Letter. You
will obferve, that I have concerned myfelf
merely with the *Principles* themfelves,—not with
the *Application* he makes of them to the American controverfy. Indeed if the Principles
cannot be fupported, the Application fails of
courfe. There are however many other things
made ufe of in the Doctor's Pamphlet, in order
to point out the injuftice of the fovereignty
claimed by Parliament over the American Co-

A   lonies,

lonies, as well as the impolicy, iniquity, dif-
honòur, and evil confequence of maintaining it
by force of arms. But neither with this, or
with that controverfy, have I meddled in the
following Obfervations. My pen has been ac-
tuated by views of a more general nature.
The cafe is this. It feems to me, that the
American pretenfions have very often been
fupported on exceeding unwarrantable and licentious principles, as well in regard to Liberty and Civil Government in general, as to
the Conftitution of this Country in particular.
To take notice of all the trafh of this kind,
that comes before the Public in a country,
where there is happily fo much legal freedom
of fpeaking and writing as in this,—would be
an idle occupation. Candor alfo will lend, in
fome cafes, the moft favorable conftruction poffible to the unguarded affertions, that feem to
proceed from a general zeal for Liberty : yet
as *there cannot be,* according to Mr. LOCKE's
remark *, *a greater mifchief to Prince and People,*
than the propagating wrong notions concerning Go-
vernment; therefore when particular circumftances mark fuch fentiments with unufual im-
portance; when they are fo determinately de-
livered as to preclude all benign interpretation;
                                           when

* On *Government,* preface.

when they are applied and afferted in fuch a manner, as to loofen the bonds of civil Society, and unfettle the juft principles, on which all civil Government and our own excellent Conftitution are founded; when they are falfely impofed upon us, as the fentiments of the moft admired writers on Government and civil Liberty, as the principles of our own conftitution, as the foundation of the Revolution and of the acceffion of the Houfe of Hanover; when they are cried up as the only foundation of all true, invaluable, unalienable LIBERTY, and every ftate, difagreeing with them, is ftigmatized with the odious name of SLAVERY;——in fuch, and fuch like circumftances, there is furely a peculiar propriety in a decent, candid, and rational oppofition to their unjuftifiable pretenfions. This I apprehend to be the cafe at prefent; and it is under a fenfe of that propriety the Obfervations here tranfmitted to you on Doctor PRICE's principles have been penned, with a view to obftruct their propagation. The uncommon fanction they have met with; the great ftrefs he himfelf lays upon them; and the literary reputation of the Author, engaged me to fet myfelf in oppofition to this publication in particular. With what fuccefs, you and my readers muft judge.

You wifh alfo to have my fentiments on the controverfy with the Colonies. If you want me to fpeak pofitively and determinately, as is the manner of fome, on every point relating to it; that is what my information, and the evidence before me, will not allow : but I will not fcruple in the leaft to communicate them to you, with that degree of evidence, they are accompanied with in my own mind, and to illuftrate and confirm them by remarks on feveral parts of Doctor PRICE's pamphlet, that relate to the fubject. I fhall devote the remaining part of this Letter to that purpofe ; defiring to keep all difcuffion, concerning the American controverfy, feparate from the fubfequent *obfervations* on his Principles of Civil Liberty and Government.

§ 1. There is not, Sir, with me the fmalleft grain of doubt of the Parliament being, to all intents and purpofes of Government, and as far as that truft extends, *fovereign and fupreme* over the whole Britifh Empire, unlefs fpecial exemptions can be produced. The Conftitution and its principles neither know, nor admit of, any other. But to fpeak, in the firft place, more particularly to the original queftion concerning Taxation ; the American Colonies afferted in 1765 as follows : " That the Taxation of the people
" by

" by themselves, or by persons chosen by them-
" selves, to represent them, is the distinguish-
" ed characteristic of British freedom." VIR-
GINIA.—" That the constitution of government
" in this province ought to be perfectly free.
" That the Taxation of the people of this pro-
" vince by any other persons whatsoever, than
" the Representatives they annually elect to
" serve as Members of Assembly, is unconsti-
" tutional and subversive of public liberty, of
" their birth-right and indubitable privileges."
PENSYLVANIA.———" That all Acts by any
" Power whatever, other than the general As-
" sembly of this province, imposing taxes on
" the inhabitants, are infringements of our in-
" herent and unalienable Rights as Men and Bri-
" tish subjects, and render void the most valu-
" able declarations of our Charter." MASSA-
CHUSETS.—" That no taxes ever have, or can
" be constitutionally imposed on the people of
" these Colonies, but by their respective Le-
" gislatures, as being their only Representa-
" tives." CONGRESS at *New-York*. *

Thefe

---

* See these *Resolves* of those several bodies in the *Appen-
dix* to *the Controversy between Great-Britain and her Colonies
reviewed*, London, 1769.

Thefe feem to me very groundlefs pofitions. I think there cannot be a more evident truth, than that the right of taxing any part of the Britifh empire, and confequently the American Colonies, unlefs particularly exempted by grant or compact, is legally and conftitutionally refident in the Parliament. Nor do I find that the American Colonies (excepting *Maryland*) are at all exempted from this general fubjection by any charters, grants, or compacts: with that exception, the invalidity of their charters, to exempt them from Parliamentary taxation, has been clearly demonftrated by the able writer of *Remarks on the Acts of the thirteenth Parliament of Great-Britain*; and in the *Penfylvanian* charter there is a claufe clearly decifive on this point againft that province, and confequentially againft the others. I therefore conclude the Colonies, as members of the Britifh community, to be, by Law and Conftitution, fubject to the fupreme authority of Parliament in regard to taxation, juft the fame as any other part of the community. This may be *right* or *wrong* according to principles of *natural* equity;—it is neverthelefs fact; it is neverthelefs the *Law* and the *Conftitution* of the Britifh Empire.

§ 2. Much

§ 2. Much has been said on this occasion about the *Principles* of the Constitution; with a view to prove, that, according to them, the Colonies *are* or *ought* to be perfectly free, and independent of the authority of Parliament, in regard to taxation. After considerable investigation, I can find no principles in the Constitution, that imply any such thing, but many, that loudly speak the reverse. The grand topic in this line of argument is,—That *it is a principle of the British Constitution, that no British subject can be taxed but with his own consent.* If the arguments, used to support this position, be allowed, they will equally prove, that, according to the principles of the Constitution, no American subject can be bound by any law or regulation without his *own* consent,—and that the Colonies ought to be their *own legislators*, as well as their *own taxers.* Consent, whether *personal*, or by *delegation*, has no more constitutional connection with taxation, than with every other right of the supreme power. But the truth is, the position itself, as understood in this application of it, is destitute of all foundation. Like the prerogative axiom, *The King can do no wrong*, it is indeed true in a particular qualified sense of the words; but if taken literally, and strained beyond the only meaning
warranted

warranted by Law and the Conftitution, it is
falfe, and capable of very mifchievous application. If you underftand by the words *own confent*, the confent of both Houfes of Parliament,
of which the Commons are a body delegated, by
a ftated mode of election, to be the Reprefentatives of the people at large ; the maxim is perfectly agreeable to truth, and in this fenfe has
juftly been laid down as a privilege of our Government : but in that ftrict fenfe of confent,
either *perfonal*, or by a *reprefentative of one's own
choice*, in which it is applied to fupport the
American pretenfions, it is a very falfe, abfurd,
and licentious doctrine ; as I mean to have evidently fhewn in fome obfervations in the *York
Chronicle* of the 7th and 14th of April laft year,
under the fignature of LIBERIUS. The perfon, who then advanced it, being mifled by
the authority of others, was much furprized at
my requiring him to prove what he had taken
upon truft, as an uncontrovertible and univerfally acknowledged truth, and was probably
much more aftonifhed, upon muftering together
all the forces he could collect, to find that,
though otherwife good troops, they were totally infufficient for that fervice.

That

That the people of America share not so
largely as the inhabitants of England and Scot-
land in those checks or securities, which the
principles or *actual state* of our Constitution wisely
afford against the abuse of civil power in general, or of the important power of taxation in
particular,—I readily allow. Pretensions of this
kind have some foundation in equity and our
free government :—more of this presently.

§ 3. But the Leaders of the American Colonies and their advocates are not content with
such pretensions, nor with resting their more
important ones on *charters,* and the *principles of
the Constitution* ; they ascend to a higher source
than either ; they desire to bring the question
to a *higher test and surer issue,* as they term it *.
It is said to be repugnant to the *Law of Nature,*
and the *essential unalienable rights of Mankind,* that
the Colonies should be subject to taxation by
Parliamentary authority, or by any authority but
of their own general Assemblies. Now if this
be true, I am sure, that by the *same principles,*
every other right, every other power of Parliament over them, not forgetting the almost
only one now uncontested of regulating their
commerce, which some so inconsistently main-

B   tain,

* Price's *Observations on Civil Liberty, &c.* p. 32, 41.

tain, muſt fall to the ground: I contend, that the ſame *natural* principles, which prove, that the Parliament cannot have a right to tax them, will equally prove that body of men to have no manner of civil or coercive authority over them whatever. If they have a *natural unalienable* right to tax themſelves, they have the *ſame* right to govern themſelves, and regulate their own affairs, according to their own diſcretion. And in fact, to this extent do almoſt all the arguments, that have been manufactured from ſuch general principles, reach. They ſet the American part of the Empire quite afloat from the reſt, and extend to an entire civil independance. To inſtance from the grand topic of all; to wit, " that no man or number of men can, " conſiſtent with *natural right and juſtice*, be " taxed, but by the actual conſent, either of " themſelves in perſon, or of repreſentatives " choſen freely by themſelves:" now if this be granted, it is evidently equally contradictory to *natural right*, that any man, or any communities of men, ſhould be *governed* or *controlled* at all in their own concerns without ſuch actual conſent. However you underſtand, limit, or qualify that poſition, it will in the ſame ſenſe, with the ſame limits, and the ſame qualifications, apply to every act and ordinance of civil Government.

vernment. Whatever fort of confent be neceffary, by *natural right*, to the taxation of a man's
property, the very fame is equally neceffary to
any governmental difpofition over his perfon or
actions; for it has evidently no more *natural*
connection with taxation, than with every other
power of Government.

Doctor PRICE's principles of civil Liberty
go allo the fame length; which he himfelf
feems to allow in two or three places; though
he has chofen, he fays, to confine his views
(but for what reafon?) to *taxation* and
internal legiflation *: the latter is indeed now
become, by a very natural courfe of things, a
part of the queftion in difpute between this
Kingdom and the Colonies. They at firft con-
fined *their* views to the power of *taxation*; now
they extend them to *internal legiflation*. The
topics they argued from againft the former,—
and the very difagreeable exertions of Parliamentary legiflation and coercive power, confequent upon their refiftance,—naturally led to this
removal of the boundaries of the original queftion; and muft as naturally lead on their views,
as circumftances permit, to the removal of every power they judge difagreeable.

B 2

§ 4. The

* See page 37, 28, 100.

§ 4. The queſtion therefore is now, in faƐt, as DoƐtor PRICE gives it,——"Whether the "American Colonies are bound to be ſubjeƐt "to the juriſdiƐtion of the Parliament, in re- "ſpeƐt of taxation and internal legiſlation?" *
Accordingly the general *Congreſs*, held at *Phila- delphia* in 1774, aſſert,—"that as the Engliſh "Coloniſts are not, and from their local and "other circumſtances can not be, repreſented "in the Britiſh Parliament, they are entitled to "a *free* and *excluſive* power of *legiſlation* in their "ſeveral provincial legiſlatures, in all caſes of "*taxation* and *internal polity*, ſubjeƐt only to the "negative of their ſovereign," viz. the King †.

I have not, as I ſaid before, a grain of doubt about the ſovereignty and ſupremacy of the Parliament over the whole Britiſh empire, un- leſs ſpecial legal exemptions can be pleaded. This is agreeable to the Conſtitution and its principles. The American Colonies are a part of the Britiſh empire, and have no ſuch exemp- tion to plead, except *Maryland*, in point of tax- ation. On the contrary, their Charters, and
the

---

* Page 42.

† *ExtraƐts from the votes, &c. of the American Congreſs, held the 5th of September,* 1774. *Reſolve the 4th.*

the firſt ſettlements in America, bear upon the face and circumſtances of them an avowed general ſubmiſſion to the Government as by law eſtabliſhed in this country. The ſocial compact is in moſt caſes only an implied agreement; but in this it has been explicitly recognized and renewed, with certain modifications, as were judged agreeable to the circumſtances. The Coloniſts ſettled in a diſtant part of the earth, under the expreſs avowal and claim of being *Britiſh ſubjects*, members of the Britiſh community; under ſanction of the common protection and authority; under acknowledgement of a general ſubjection to the eſtabliſhed ſupreme legiſlature; under certain charters and ſtipulations ſettled by the legal powers then exiſting;—which charters and ſtipulations not only in themſelves implicitly ſuppoſe, but contain expreſs reſerve of, their remaining under the authority of the one common ſupreme Legiſlative. Nothing can be more evident, than that ſuch tranſactions as theſe ſpeak aloud very plainly the ſubjection of the Coloniſts to Parliament, in regard to every branch of civil power, from which they are not by grant or charter exempted. And accordingly it has conſtantly and uninterruptedly exerciſed all ſuch legiſlative and governmental powers, as have been judged

expedient,

expedient, in all forts of concerns; and alfo
enforced this its own conftitutional right and
fupremacy over the Colonies, by an exprefs ftatute in King William the *third*'s time, when
fome feeble attempts were made againft it.
" When Lord Chatham," fays the noted JUNI-
us, " affirms that the authority of the Britifh
" legiflature is not fupreme over the Colonies,
" in the *fame* fenfe, in which it is fupreme over
" Great Britain,—I liften to *him* with diffidence
" and refpect, but without the fmalleft degree
" of conviction or affent." *

This being clearly the cafe,—the leaders and
advocates of our fellow-fubjects in America en-
deavour to turn our views now entirely from
thofe tranfactions and the Colonial charters to
other

* *Letters*, &c. vol. II. p. 268. Dr. PRICE afks, p. 40,
" Did they not fettle in America under the faith of Char-
" ters?" Doubtlefs; and this Country claims their fubordination to Parliament under the *faith* of thofe *Charters*.—
" Did not thefe Charters promife them the enjoyment of
" all the rights of Englifhmen?" None inconfiftent with
the fovereign fupremacy of Parliament; no *exclufive* right
of felf-legiflation and felf-taxation by their own Affemblies: that would imply a contradiction. For the reft, the
allowing them to tax themfelves, and to have fubordinate
local legiflatures of their own, excludes not in the leaft the
fupreme authority of Parliament.

other more pliable principles; faying, " that
the fupreme authority of Parliament over the
Colonies is contrary to right and juftice, and
therefore never could be eftablifhed by any
compact, ftipulations, or acquiefcence:"—" Had
" there been," fays Doctor PRICE, " exprefs fti-
" pulations to this purpofe in all the charters
" of the Colonies, they would, in my opinion,
" be no more bound by them, than if it had
" been ftipulated with them, that they fhould
" go naked, or expofe themfelves to the incur-
" fions of wolves and tigers.——The queftion
" with all liberal enquirers ought to be, not
" what jurifdiction over them *Precedents, Sta-*
" *tutes,* and *Charters* give, but what reafon and
" equity, and the rights of humanity give." *

Thus we are got again to principles of *natural right :* and I anfwer again, that according
to thefe, the Doctor fhould have *extended* his
views further than to *taxation* and *internal legiflation* †: for thefe fame principles will equally
prove the Parliament to have no civil authority
whatever over the Colonies. They have as good
a *natural* right to regulate their own trade, and
their

* Page 41, 32.
† Page 100, in the *New.*

their own connections with other states, as to be
their own internal legislators. Accordingly Mr.
MOLYNEUX, when he argued against *Ireland's*
being bound by Acts of the British Parliament,
on the principle,—" that the Irish had no *share*.
" in making those laws, and that Slavery is the
" being bound by laws to which we do not
" consent" (the very principles adopted by
Doctor PRICE *), very consistently denied the
Parliament's right to make any laws, even to
regulate the trade of Ireland ;—in this much
more fair and consistent than the present asser-
tors of those principles in favour of America,
who still maintain the Parliament of Great-Britain to have rights over the people of America,
which those very principles clearly subvert.—
One writer indeed scruples not to speak out in
the following manner :—" Many will perhaps
" be surprized to see the legislative authority
" of the British Parliament over the Colonies,
" denied *in every instance*. Those the Writer
" informs, that, when he began this piece, he
" would probably have been surprized at such
" an opinion himself. For it was the result,
" not the occasion of his disquisitions. He en-
" tered upon them with a view and expecta-
" tion of being able to trace some *constitutional*
line

" *line* between thofe cafes, in which we (the
" *Americans*) ought, and thofe, in which we
" ought not, to acknowledge the power of Par-
" liament over us. In the profecution of his
" inquiries, he became fully convinced, that
" *fuch a line doth not exift*; and that there can be
" *no medium* between *acknowledging* and *denying*
" that power in ALL CASES." *

§ 5. You will probably fay, that I have hitherto only explained to you my opinion, that
the arguments from *natural right*, in favour of
the American pretenfions, extend to entire political independence,—without telling you my
fenfe of their intrinfic merit and validity. It is
true. I meant to infinuate, that as the Colonies are *faid* ftill to acknowledge their rightful
fubjection to parliamentary authority, in regard
to the regulation of trade and other civil concerns, as ufual before the prefent troubles,—
therefore thofe topics from the Law of Nature
would prove *too much*, and confequently *nothing*.
But I will anfwer you more directly. I find no
efficacy at all in thofe *general* reafonings hither-

C   to

* *Confiderations on the nature, and the extent of the legiflative authority of the Britifh Parliament.* Printed in 1774,
attributed to Dr. FRANKLIN. See Dr. TUCKER's 5th tract,
p. 47.

to alledged to prove their having any *natural*,
much lefs a *conftitutional*, right to Self-govern-
ment and Independence on the authority of
Parliament, in any one department of civil
power : indeed they all center in Doctor PRICE's
principles of Government and Civil Liberty,
the infufficiency of which I have endeavoured
to point out in the piece that accompanies this
letter.

There is however, in my opinion, a good
deal more appearance of plaufibility in fome
hints and argumentations, occafionally thrown
out only as collateral fupports, founded upon
the *particular fituation* and *fpecial circumftances*
of the cafe : as for inftance ;—the Colonies being grown to a body of powerful States, likely
to become very foon a mighty empire, equal
and haply fuperior to Great Britain ; able in
every refpect to fubfift alone, to act for and
protect themfelves, and feparated from us by a
great Ocean, at the diftance of above 3000
miles. Muft fuch an Empire, it may be faid,
fo circumftanced, which from its peculiar and
diftant fituation from Great Britain, has neceffarily fuch different natural connections and interefts, and alfo wants thofe ties of near neigh-
bourfhip with it, that ordinarily connect people
together

together into one civil community, under one
and the fame Legiflature,—ftill continue, to its
own evident inconvenience, united to Great
Britain as *one* State? Nay! is it not a ftill
greater impropriety and inconvenience,—that
fuch an empire, fo circumftanced, fhould be
fubject to a Legiflature, refident at fo great a
diftance, on this fide the Atlantic, with the
members of which, in general, the connections
muft unavoidably be very loofe, the intercourfe
difficult and tedious, the fellow-feeling and
mutual fenfibility too faint;—can fuch a Legiflature, fo circumftanced, fuperintend adequate-
ly and beneficially a Community fo remote;
can it be a competent judge of their circumftances and abilities, of their fufferings and op-
preffions; can it quickly enough know, feel,
or redrefs evils, and operate as the public welfare may require? Have not the American
communities therefore a well-grounded plea in
reafon and equity to emancipate themfelves
from civil union with us, and to govern themfelves? efpecially as it is much to be doubted,
whether even any fcheme can be devifed of
uniting them under one Legiflature with us,
confiftent with a due regard to the principles of
a free and equal Government*. We were,

* I fincerely hope this pofition may be found groundlefs.

they may fay, in our infancy and firft youth, under the care of our parents; and during that time fubfervient to their interefts, under their authority; now we are arrived at manhood, and ought to be, from ftrength and fituation, independent agents.

This mode of argumentation, in favour of the propriety and juftice of American *independence*, is fuggefted by Doctor PRICE; but I think I have placed it in a much more forcible light, than it is found in his pamphlet *. I would, in the firft place, obferve, that the point here argued, not being part of the queftion between this Kingdom and the Colonies, is out of the line of the prefent fubject. No fuch claim has yet been made in *direct* terms. When it is, it will be time to confider this particular argument more fully. In the mean time, admitting at prefent the apparent plaufibility of it,—fuch arguers fhould be reminded, that in their zeal for the interefts of our brethren in America, they entirely overlook the *intereft* that *Great Britain* may have in the continuance of the civil compact, which unites it with the Colonies.

Civil

* See page 19, 20, 27, 33, 44.

Civil Society would be a mere rope of fand, if every individual, or whole bodies of men, had a difcretionary liberty to diffolve their civil union with the reft of the community, whenever they judged it moft for their convenience. Such a liberty would be evidenly inconfiftent with the ends of Civil Society. The *private* interefts indeed of individuals, or of particular bodies of individuals, may juftly be confidered, as the *motive* of affociating with others, but can not be the *meafure* of their obligations to the Society: for other people had the fame views in affociating with them, and thus the *common intereft* becomes the end and bond of the union, and the ftandard of political duty. Protection and fecurity is what the Society gives. Allegiance is what it has a right to, and can not fubfift without. There is thus a mutual compact between all the members of a community, and between the body politic and the members; a mutual intereft in each other, which is particularly modified by the various relations the different parts of the whole ftand in to one another, arifing from fituation, agreement, or other circumftances. And doubtlefs *particular* circumftances and fitua·ions may enhance prodigiously the degree of that intereft in the common union: as for inftance, the neighbourhood

bourhood of potent ftates animated with a fpirit of dominion and encroachment; wealth and
ftrength expended by the community on any
particular part; a common debt; any common
obligation incumbent upon the whole fociety;—
which things I only juft hint at in the utmoft
generality, but are capable of being much more
ftrongly urged. It appears plainly, however,
that Civil Society, being formed for mutual
benefit, implies a mutual contract and allegiance; from which one part may not difcretion-
ally depart, merely for their own private convenience, without content of the reft; and that
there may be very juft and weighty reafons
for refufing affent in fuch a cafe, and forcing
the refractory part to due fubordination.

Now it is a *fact*, that Great-Britain and the
American Colonies are one Civil community.
The Charters implied the original compact, and
were alfo a formal renewal of it with peculiar
circumftances and modifications, according to
which they varioufly contribute, in their refpec-
tive eftablifhed order and relation, to the good,
fafety, and welfare of the whole Empire. Thefe
bonds,—this obligation,—may not be diffolved
merely at the pleafure and for the particular
convenience of one party. How far this country

try may be particularly interefted from fuch circumftances as above hinted at, or others of like nature, to keep the Colonies within the bonds and terms of the mutual compact, I leave to the judgment of others ;——meaning only to fuggeft, that thefe confiderations ought at leaft to be *put in the fcale*, when people are weighing arguments for the *independance* of the Colonies, founded on their particularcir cumftances, diftinct interefts, greater conveniency, flourifhing ftate, ability to do without us, and fuch like *private* motives.

Circumftances may doubtlefs be *imagined* and *conceived*, in which the American Colonies, as well as any other part of the Empire, might juftly claim emancipation. Accordingly Doctor PRICE enters with this view into the fpeculative region of poffibles *; where it is to no purpofe to purfue, till thofe circumftances become actual, or are declared fo by him.

§ 6. But, Sir! although the claims of the Colonies to be fubject only to their own Affemblies in matters of legiflation and taxation, or in any department of civil fovereignty, ftand not on any reafonable ground; although the supreme

* See page 43—45.

supreme authority of Parliament over the whole British Empire be an incontestible axiom, according to *law* and the *principles* of the *Constitution*;—yet it must be acknowledged that the case of the Colonies, in regard to this Legislative body, is very materially different from that of the inhabitants of Great Britain. The particular relation, in which that Legislature stands to the latter, forms, and was intended to form, a considerable check to the abuse of the supreme trust of government, and of that important branch of it—*Taxation*. This is *one* characteristic of our Constitution, as far as it is a free one. The House of Commons is a temporary body, elected every seven years, or sooner, by the Freeholders of forty shillings a year throughout the kingdom, and by the Burgesses of cities and boroughs scattered all over the kingdom,—the members of which are subject to the same laws and taxes they impose upon others, and are settled in all parts of the country; intimately connected with it and with the rest of the people, by their families, estates, connections, dependencies, &c.; which is the case likewise with the Peers.

Widely different is doubtless the case of those large communities of British subjects,

fituated in America. They are deftitute of thofe
controls on the fupreme legiflature, which arife
from the rights and circumftances juft mentioned: for that power is fixed on this fide the
Atlantic, at 3000 miles diftance from them;
they fhare not any wife in that power, neither
perfonally, nor by their votes or intereft at
elections; neither do they ftand in thofe other
circumftances above-mentioned of near connection with the Legiflators; they might therefore perhaps have reafon to apprehend a dif-
proportionate part of the public burden being
caft upon them, for the eafe of us and the legiflators themfelves.—This difference is very
feelingly reprefented by a writer, whofe words
I fhall infert below *; and Doctor Price's few
D   reflections

---

* " Do you not know the infinite difference between a
" nation, where *all* have *not* the power of voting for their
" reprefentatives, and a nation where *none have* that power?
" The former is *your* condition, and therefore, you are a
" free people; the former is what we claim: the latter is
" the condition of flaves, and that is what you offer us.—
" England can not be taxed, but by an Affembly, where
" her land is reprefented by knights, her monied intereft
" by citizens and burgeffes, and therefore fhe is a free na-
" tion. Is then America on a par with England, in point
" of freedom, if fhe can be taxed by an Affembly, to which
" her Freeholders fend *no* Knights, and her Cities *no* Citi-
" zens?

reflections to the fame purpofe muft therefore be allowed their due weight. *

Thefe

" zens ?----It is not true, that we are in *as good* a condition
" as thofe Britons, whom you call unreprefented, and who
" are not electors : for even *they* have this great advantage,
" that both the reprefentative, and the electors, pay a part
" of the tax, as well as thofe, who have no fuffrage ; where-
" as, if the Houfe of Commons of England fhould tax the
" Americans, neither the reprefentatives, nor the electors,
" would pay any proportion of what they impofed upon
" us ; they would not tax, but *untax* themfelves. The
" condition therefore of an Englifhman, who has no fuf-
" frage, when taxed by the Britifh legiflature, and of an
" American taxed by the fame authority, are totally diffi-
" milar. - - - - A body of 500 men, fituated in the midft of
" feven millions, and taxing thofe feven millions, would
" furely be more bound to moderation, by fear, if not by
" principle, than the fame body, affifted and fupported by
" thofe feven millions, in taxing two millions, who are at
" a diftance. To opprefs, in one inftance, would, at leaft,
" be infamy, if it would not be punifhment ; in the other,
" they might find it popularity, they might think it patrio-
" tifm. Mr. P—TT faid (if I miftake not) that every man
" in England could huzza at an election : even that method
" of expreffing one's wifhes, is fome fatisfaction, and has
" fome influence ; the fhoutings of the people have had
" great effects ;—We can not even *huzza* at an election.----
" How different is the effect of a petition prefented by the
" hands

These comparative difadvantages of the American Colonies have arifen accidentally from their emigration ; but they have not, till lately, been of age or ftrength enough to feel them fo univerfally :—from feeling they have proceeded to reafoning; and a concurrence of various circumftances has extended their views to unwarranted lengths. But indeed fo far as they only defire to be put upon a more *equal* footing with ourfelves, in regard to government and conftitutional checks againft the abufes of power, efpecially in regard to taxation, I really think them warranted by the principle of equity, liberty, and the fpirit of the Britifh conftitution. I earneftly wifh them to be put upon as equal a footing as poffible with their fellow-fubjects in Britain. How far, and

D 2 in

" hands of the injured, enforced by their affiduity, and
" recommended by their tears, from that of our *paper-re-*
" *prefentations?* They are fubject to be mifreprefented in
" a thoufand ways : they come cold, and you do not feel
" them ; often too late, and you cannot comply with them ;
" and what was done by you through inattention and mif-
" take, muft be maintained *for dignity*; in a word, they
" do not ftrike home, either upon your caution, or your
" kindnefs; your affections or your fears: In this particu-
" lar, the very women and children of England have an
" influence upon Parliament, of which the Americans are
" deftitute. How different is your Lot from ours!" *Cafe
of Great-Britain and America*, London 1769, p. 6—15.

in what degree or mode, this be practicable, confiftent with the being united under one fupreme authority,—is a fubject, I prefume, of fome difficulty, but not impoffible to be adjufted, were there mutual good difpofitions on both fides. Several fchemes have been propofed: the Parliament made an offer to this purpofe, in regard to the great object of taxation, in the fpring of laft year:—it was this; " *that up-* " *on acts of their own legiflation for raifing a rea-* " *fonable fum towards the charges, with which* " *government muft neceffarily be burdened for their* " *protection and defence, acts of Parliament for* " *taxing them ought to be repealed, and that it will* " *not be advifeable to tax them for the future.*"

This was putting them nearly on the footing of Ireland. How has it been received? With infult. If the American Colonies did not like that,—fhould they not, in their turn, have propofed fome other fcheme? But it is remarkable, that while many plans have been devifed here, in order to do them as much juftice as poffible, they keep quite aloof, without offering any terms tending to reconcile our mutual union under one fupreme authority with their fecurity and freedom. The truth of the matter is,—the prefent ideas there allow of no fuch conciliation:

conciliation : *union* with us un..er *one common
supreme authority* is what neither their leaders,
nor Doctor PRICE's princi, les, will admit of;
" the Colonies infift," fays he, " on being *treat-
" ed as free communities :"* but inftead of faying
fo in direct terms, they offer nothing in anfwer
to our condefcenfions,—but the demand to be
reftored to the fame fituation and connections
with Great Britain, as at the clofe of the laft
war; that is, according to their ideas, to a
ftate of EXCLUSIVE *internal legiflation* and *taxation* by their own Affemblies, which they abfolutely infift upon ; that is, demanding, that
Parliament fhall renounce all the claims, that
gave occafion to, or increafed, the prefent troubles, while they peremptorily refufe to recede
an inch from theirs : it is demanding, in regard
to taxation and the public burdens, that we,
and the reft of this great empire, fhould place
an implicit confidence in *their difcretion*, at
the fame time they abfolutely refufe to place
any in *ours* :—it is demanding, not to be put
on an *equal* footing with other Britifh fubjects,
but on a *mere independent* one ; on fuch a footing, as is inconfiftent with their remaining Britifh fubjects. To fuch demands the Colonies
have no legal, conftitutional, or natural right :

reafon

* See page 56.

reafon and equity alfo pronounce fuch claims
to be equally inadmiffible by this country and
the Parliament, as the claim to their abfolute
fubmiffion could be to them. Accordingly the
Parliament, at the fame time that it held out
the olive branch in the refolution of the fpring
1775, declared it could not relinquifh any part
of its fovereign authority over all the dominions
of the Britifh empire.

In fhort, any terms they claim for further
fecurity againft oppreffion, or the equitable in-
creafe of freedom, confiftent with our joint and
equal fubmiffion to the one fupreme legiflature,
ought to be duly attended to,—and are a fuit-
able ground to treat upon ; but fuch as deftroy
this bond of civil union, and vindicate to them
felf-legiflation and felf-taxation, independent
of the authority of Parliament, overfhoot the
mark much too far.

§ 7. See there, Sir! my fentiments on the
principal queftions relating to the power of
Parliament over the American part of the Britifh empire. Others have been ftarted concerning the *policy* and *propriety* of the exertions
of that power in particular inftances of taxation, legiflation, coercion, or the oppofing force

to

to their refiftance. I do not think myfelf qualified, either by fufficient knowledge of particular facts, or by infight enough into the in-
terior ftate, trade, production, finances, and
refources of the Colonies, perhaps not of this
country, to communicate a fatisfactory judgment on thofe topics :—they have been largely
difcuffed, though with a latitude, that allows
many plaufible things to be alledged on both
fides, with much wrangling and fpeculation
to little purpofe. One thing however feems
to admit not of difpute ; to wit, that the American Colonies *ought* to bear a proportionable
part of the public burdens of the ftate. This
is evident on general principles : I need not
therefore urge, that half the prefent burthen-
fome debt on the ftate was contracted in a war,
begun in their immediate defence, and profe-
cuted with the utmoft zeal and vigour, till its
good fuccefs iffued in delivering them from a
moft dangerous and obnoxious neighbour, and
in enabling them, by all the great advantages
confequent thereupon,—to bid defiance to us
and the fupreme Legiflature. Some feem to
think, that no profit ought to be expected
from the Colonies, but what refults from com-
mercial regulations. How great the profits are
which the ftate derives from the Act of Navi-
gation

gation in all its confequences, I pretend not to
afcertain; but I fhould apprehend, with fubmiffion to better judgment, that a *proportionable taxation* would be as beneficial a mode of
their contributing to the common fund,—and
certainly a lefs arbitrary and oppreffive one,—
than fuch a *monopoly of their commerce:* I am
aware of the general opinion, that the manu-
factures of this country, and by their means,
its wealth and flourifhing ftate, are principally
fupported by that monopoly; but I doubt the
fact, and am neverthelefs of opinion, that the
people of this ifland would be more laftingly,
fecurely, and fubftantially benefited by the
other mode, and allowing the Colonifts in general as free a trade, as we ourfelves enjoy
here.

In regard to the *right* and *propriety* of ufing
coercive meafures againft the American refiftance to government,—I can fee no reafon
to doubt either. This country and the colonies are united in one civil community,—under one fupreme legiflature,—for the purpofe
of the general welfare. To this union the
Colonies now run counter; by rejecting the
fupreme authority of that legiflature in fome
of the moft effential departments of civil government;

vernment; by refuſing to be ſubject, in thoſe
reſpects, to any common joint Legiſlature,—to
any power but their own provincial Aſſemblies.
Suppoſe the cities of London, Briſtol, or Leeds
were to deny the right of Parliament to tax
their citizens, and pretend to the right of ſelf-
legiſlation and taxation, independent of its authority, and *inſiſt*, as Doctor Price ſays the
Colonies do, on *being treated as free communities;* *—ſhould you not think that it would be
the right, as well as the duty of Parliament, in
truſt for the reſt of the community, to compel
them to due ſubordination, and puniſh them,
as circumſtances ſhould require, for diſobedi-
ence?   Apply this to the American Colonies.
The pretenſions they form to ſelf-government
and ſelf-taxation by their own Aſſemblies, independent of Parliamentary authority, are,
agreeable to what has been ſaid in the forego-
ing pages, equally unjuſtifiable and inadmiſſi-
ble as in any other part of the ſtate.   What
remains then for the ſupreme power to do, in
conformity with its truſt, but to compel them
to their duty and the terms of the ſocial compact?   The reſt of the community has a contracted right to their equal ſubordination, and
Parliament is obliged to enforce it;—particu-

E   larly

* See page 56.

larly fo as not to leave their contributions to
the public burdens of the ftate to their own
difcretion, to *give* and *grant* as they pleafe. At
the fame time every well-difpofed perfon will
heartily wifh, that no private interefts, or ill
temper on either fide, may prevent the conteft
being ended and the fword fheathed, as foon as
ever the interefts of the nation, of juftice, and
of humanity, will allow, with every fecurity to
their property and civil rights confiftent with
the general welfare.

As to particular meafures of Adminiftration
in thefe matters, either prior or fubfequent to
the refiftance the Colonies have made to Government,—I did not take up my pen with a
view to fay any thing about them, but only to
give you, in compliance with your defire, my
fentiments on the pretenfions of the American
Colonies, in refpect of Right and Equity, accompanied with a little fpice of reafoning, and,
I hope, with acceptable moderation and candor.

I proceed now to communicate fome brief remarks on feveral paffages in Doctor PRICE's
pamphlet, which will illuftrate and confirm the
preceding fentiments.

§ 8. In

§ 8. In order to render the Parliamentary authority of internal legiſlation and taxation over the Colonies odious, the Doctor miſrepreſents its nature and the nature of Civil Government very groſsly. He repreſents it,—as a *diſturbance of*, and an *attack upon*, *the poſſeſſion of their property*; as ſuch an *abſolute command*, *mere diſcretionary power*, *and eternal maſtery*, *over their whole property* and *legiſlation*, *as would leave them nothing to call their own*;—as a power of *ſubjecting them to any modes of government at pleaſure*, for inſtance, to the *arbitrary power of the crown*, or of *ceding them to France*;—in ſhort, as a power, *to which it is impoſſible to fix any bounds or limitations*; a power of *doing with them juſt what we pleaſe*, ſo that their ſtate is that of *unconditional ſubmiſſion and ſlavery*, of *having no law but our will*, *no right of judging*, *how far authority in legiſlation and taxation may extend*, but *holding all that is valuable at the diſcretion of another.* *

This is doubtleſs a dreadful picture; and though ſome of the expreſſions are capable of a favourable meaning, yet taking the whole together, and the ſenſe, which the different parts mutually impart to one another, it muſt

E 2   be

* See page 19, 26, 34, 35, 39, 40, 43, 44, 45, 47, 53, 60, 61, 62, 89, 101.

be allowed to be a complete defcription of the
moft arbitrary Defpotifm on the one hand, and
of the moft abject Slavery on the other. But
it is happily a very extravagant mifreprefentation of the nature of the cafe ; and the relation
between Governors and the governed, in any
of the Doctor's free ftates, might be carica-
tured juft in the fame terms.

The power, which is claimed by the Legiflature over the Colonies can not, as Dr. PRICE
obferves, be better ftated than in the words of
an act of Parliament made on purpofe to define
it *. That act declares, " That this kingdom
" has power, and of right ought to have power,
" to make laws and ftatutes to bind the Colo-
" nies and people of America in all cafes what-
" ever." *Dreadful power indeed!* exclaims the
Doctor, *I defy any one to exprefs Slavery in ftronger language.*—Yes! I think that vile ftate has
been much ftronger expreffed by himfelf in the
terms juft mentioned. *It is the fame,* fays he,
with declaring, " that we have a right to do with
" them what we pleafe :"—That I deny : it ex-
preffes only *civil* power ; fo that the nature of
the fubject naturally limits the fenfe of the general expreffion, *all cafes whatever* ; by which
nothing

* See page 34.

nothing more was or could be meant, than that
the fupreme authority of Parliament over the
Colonies is as general, as that of Civil Government, limited by no peculiar or particular ex-
ceptions whatever. *

The truth is, that the claim of Parliament is
only to *civil* power: now Civil power, even in
the higheft and moft abfolute degree, is a truft,
limited in its own nature by the end and purpofes of the civil union, which is the fecurity
and promotion of the general welfare: beyond
thefe limits Governors have no rights, and the
People, ftrictly fpeaking, owe no fubjection.
This power is therefore not arbitrary or tyrannical in itfelf, nor implies any right of doing
with fubjects and their properties according to
mere pleafure; that would be afcribing to government a right to defeat the very end for
which it is eftablifhed, and to betray the truft
repofed

* Mr. Locke declares,——" that the *Legiflative* is, in
" all cases, whilft the Government fubfifts, supreme."
On *Government*, book II. § 150.—Thefe are the terms of
the Declaratory Act; and they fhew with what truth and
propriety Doctor Price prides himfelf on teaching the fame
doctrine with that excellent writer. This *civil omnipotence*
of Government is maintained by all the moft efteemed
writers on the fubject. Nay, the denial of it implies a
contradiction.

repofed in it. Men carry rights with them into civil fociety, which no government may in-
fringe: " The fupreme power," fays LOCKE,
" in whatever hands it be placed, is not, nor
" can poffibly be, abfolutely *arbitrary* over the
" lives and fortunes of the people. For it be-
" ing but the joint power of every member of
" the fociety, delegated to that perfon or affem-
" bly, which is legiflator; it can be no more than
" thofe perfons had in a ftate of nature, before
" they entered into fociety, and gave up to the
" community. For no body can transfer to
" another more power, than he has in himfelf;
" and no body has an abfolute arbitrary power
" over himfelf, or over any other, to deftroy his
" own life, or take away the life and proper-
" ty of another. ------ The legiflative power,
" in the utmoft bounds of it, is *limited to the*
" *public good* of the fociety. It is a power, that
" hath no other end but prefervation, and there-
" fore can never have right to deftroy, enflave,
" or defignedly to impoverifh the fubjects. ----
" The legiflative can not transfer the power of
" making laws to any other hands. For it be-
" ing but a delegative power from the people,
" they, who have it, can not pafs it over to
" others. Being derived from the people by a
" pofitive voluntary grant and inftitution, it
" can

" can be no other, than what that pofitive grant
" conveyed, which being only to make *Laws*,
" and not to make *Legiflators*, the Legiflative
" can have no power to transfer their authori-
" ty of making laws, and place it in other
" hands." *

I therefore conclude, that Doctor PRICE's
ftate of the queftion between us and the Colonies, *page* 43, to wit,—" Whether the Britifh
" Parliament has, or has not, of right, a power
" to difpofe of their property, and to model,
" as it pleafes, their governments,"—is fome-
what inaccurately and invidioufly expreffed: it
fhould have been more fairly ftated, thus ;——
Whether the Britifh Parliament has, or has not,
the *fame* right to tax their property, and to
model their governments, as it has in refpect
of any other part of the community, for the
general benefit.   But the Doctor objects,——
" that the claiming a *right* to alter the conftitutions of the Colonies implies a right of fub-
jecting them to the arbitrary power of a King,
or of the Grand Signior." †   This is afferting,
in direct contradiction to LOCKE and reafon,
that a power delegated to certain perfons, to
make

* On *Government*, book II. § 135, 141.

† See page 45, 48.

make laws, govern a ftate, and regulate all fubordinate jurifdictions and conftitutions, — implies a right to transfer that entrufted power to
other hands; an affertion, too favourable to
arbitrary power to be admitted without fub-
ftantial proof.

The Doctor however urges,—that if the *declaratory* act of Parliament above-mentioned
" means any thing, it means, that the proper-
" ty, and the legiflations of the Colonies, are
" fubject to the abfolute difcretion of Great
" Britain, and ought of right to be fo. · The
" nature of the thing admits of no limitation.
" The Colonies can never be admitted to be
" judges, how far the authority over them in
" thefe cafes fhall extend. This would be to
" deftroy it entirely. If *any* part of their pro-
" perty is fubject to our difcretion, the *whole*
" muft be fo. If we have a right to interfere
" at all in their internal legiflations, we have a
" right to interfere as far as we think proper.
" It is felf-evident, that this leaves them no-
" thing they can call their own." *—How is it
poffible that Doctor Price can reafon thus!
The moft arbitrary defpot of Afia could not
wifh for a logic more favorable to the moft ab-
                                                    ject

* See page 35.

ject flavery. The following brief obfervations will fufficiently expofe its abfurdity, without taking any further notice of the impropriety of fubftituting *Great Britain* and *us* for the *Parliament*. Government is a general difcretionary truft of command over the actions, concerns, property, and ftrength of thofe, who belong to the community, for the purpofes of the civil union. This the act declares to be vefted in the Parliament in regard to the Colonies. They are declared to be fubject to its difcretionary government, juft as we are; juft as every civil community is fubject to fome fupreme Legiflature. The nature of things admits of and neceffarily implies palpable limitations, viz.—the *ends* of the *truft*,—the *laws* of *reafon* and *nature*. The Colonies are judges, and fo are we and every people on the face of the earth, in all cafes, when oppreffed by a tyrannical exertion of authority; nor does this deftroy or impair at all the authoritative exertions of the fupreme Power within the limits of its truft; and beyond thofe limits it has, properly fpeaking, no exiftence. The great mafters of the fubject of Civil Government, the incomparable Locke and Hoadley, efpecially the latter, have fet this matter in the cleareft light, againft all the fubtilties and fophifms, that the wit of man

F   could

could invent; and have evidently fhewn, that a
right to tax or to exercife any civil power, which
is always a fiduciary truft, implies no fuch confequences as Doctor Price here infers. Indeed
he himfelf, in another place, fufficiently ener-
vates thofe abfurd inferences, by remarking,—
" that Government is an inftitution for the be-
" nefit of the people governed;------in the
" very nature of it, a trust; and all its powers
" a delegation for gaining particular ends.
" This truft may be mifapplied and abufed. It
" may be employed to defeat the very ends,
" for which it was inftituted; and to fubvert
" the very rights, which it ought to protect. --
----- " Nothing therefore can be more abfurd
" than the doctrine, which fome have taught
" with refpect to the omnipotence of Parlia-
" ments. They poffefs no power beyond the
" limits of the truft, for the execution of which
" they were formed. If they contradict this
" truft, they betray their conftituents, and dif-
" folve themfelves." *   Thus juftly can Doctor
Price reafon on this fubject, when it fuits his
purpofe! †   When he fees fit to object to the
supreme

* See page 12, 15.
† And yet even here, in this paffage, his zeal againft
fome people has led him palpably to mifunderftand the doctrine

fupreme authority of Parliament over the Colonies,—then Government is reprefented as " an
" *arbitrary* and *unlimitable defpotifm*, to which no
" people can be lawfully fubjected:" when the

uncon-

trine concerning the *omnipotence* of Parliament, and alfo to
fall inadvertently into an abfurdity by what he immediately
fubjoins. By that *omnipotence* the Doctor here means,——a
power or right extenfive beyond the limits of the truft for
which it was delegated :—now in the *firft* place, although
people may differ, more or lefs, about the general or conftitutional limits of the fupreme power of Parliament, yet I
prefume I may fafely defy him to produce an example of
any *fuch* abfurd doctrine being taught, as that of the Parliament's Authority extending beyond the limits of its truft;
and *fecondly*, Omnipotence, in this affumed fenfe, can no
more be afcribed to legiflative authority in the people
(which he fcruples not to do in the next paragraph) than to
the Parliament: for legiflative authority in the people has
the fame general and intrinfic limits, beyond which it can
not rightfully act. Indeed when he immediately fubjoins ;
" theirs is the only *real* omnipotence,"—that is felf-evident
and admits of no reply; that fort of *phyfical* omnipotence
fuperfedes effectually all right, government, and authority.

By the *omnipotence* of Parliament, which has been perti-
nently urged on feveral occafions, is meant nothing more,—
than that it is *abfolutely fupreme* in command; that there is
no *civil* or *legal* power in the ftate *fuperior* to it, and that
its acts can not be controlled or annulled by any other *authority*. This does not preclude in the leaft its being limited,

as

uncontrovertible doctrine of the *civil supremacy*
or *omnipotence* of Parliament and of the sovereign
authority is in his way,—then Government is
represented as " a *trust* and *delegation* for par-
" ticular

as to the extent of its power, either by laws of Nature, or
by rules and principles of the Constitution: it only means,
that as the Parliament is the supreme power in the state,
there neither is, nor can be, any appeal against its oppres-
sions or transgressions of those limits, but to the *natural* rights
of the people to resist oppression, injustice, and unauthorized
power.   It is the same with every civil Government on the
face of the earth: nothing is more evident to those, that
have considered the subject, than that there must be in every
civil society a supreme commanding authority, vested some-
where, over the *will, persons, concerns,* and *power* of the
whole body, for the purposes of the civil union ; and con-
sequently that the supreme Legislative, as such, is absolute,
resistible, uncontrolable, and omnipotent, viz. in relation
to the community : it is always limited by *natural* law ; it
may be limited by *constitutional* law ;—but it must be, as
Mr. LOCKE observes, in all cases, as long as the government subsists, SUPREME over every other person, body, or
power in the State : on *Government*, § 150.   This is the
doctrine of the *civil supremacy* or *omnipotence* of Government
taught by that great man, by GROTIUS, PUFFENDORF,
HUTCHESON, HOADLEY, &c.   Compare Sir EDWARD
COKE's *Institutes* iv. 36, and BLACKSTONE's *Commentaries,*
book I. chap. ii. §. 3.   How strangely has this plain evident doctrine been lately misconceived, misrepresented, and
abused by an intemperate spirit of party !

" ticular ends, beyond the limits of which it has
" no power." In both cafes, however, thefe
contradictory reprefentations are equally appo-
fite,—that is, nothing to the purpofe.

§ 9. Whether any perfons have argued for
the claims of Parliament from the neceffary
Unity of the Britifh empire, or from the *Superiority* or *Parency* of this State, in the manner
ftated by Doctor Price *, I will not ftay to ex-
amine ; though I can not think that any body
has. But certainly there is no force in any of
the arguments, which he reprefents as drawn
from thole topics ; fo that they afford him an
eafy triumph, and an opportunity of faying feveral general things little to the purpofe. Indeed the Doctor but too often widely mifrepre-
fents or mifconceives the notions and reafonings
of thofe, whom he has chofen to oppofe.

That in order to preferve the *Unity* of the
Britifh empire, there muft be lodged *fomewhere*
a power of fupreme legiflation †,—is an incon-
teftible truth : but where that is lodged, how
it is conftituted, and in what manner limited,
nobody, that knows what he is about, will at-
tempt to fhew from any general notions of
Unity,

Unity, but from the hiftory of this people and of the conftitution of their Government.

As to arguing from the *Superiority* of the *Bri-tifb State*, as Doctor PRICE terms it *,—it would be talking nonfenfe; becaufe the Colonies are a *part* of the *Britifb State*. If, by this latter term, that part called Great Britain be meant; there is no *civil* fuperiority, that I know of, claimed by this country over the Colonies; and, as to any other, it is out of the queftion.

The circumftance of our being the *parent ftate*, no more than that of our having *protected* the Colonies, can have been alledged to fhew the *conflitutional power* of Parliament;—but may poffibly, and not improperly, have been con-trafted with the unfriendly and refractory be-haviour of thofe our fellow-fubjects on the other fide the Atlantic.

§ 10. The argument for the fovereign fu-premacy of Parliament urged by fome, as Doc-tor PRICE reprefents it,—" from the land, on " which the Colonifts fettled, being ours," †— is of more force, when fairly and properly ftated, than he apprehends. The cafe is brief-ly

* See page 36.   † See page 39.

ly this. That territory, as far as it has been taken poſſeſſion of, inhabited, and ſettled in, by Britiſh ſubjects, under the authority, the ſanction, the protection, and the laws of the Britiſh ſtate, is become part of the territory of that ſtate ;— and, in this ſenſe, if you pleaſe, is *our* land, juſt as we ſay, that London is *our* capital.—It is thus, that the land of the American Provinces firſt came, and is now, by long preſcription, under the territorial ſovereignty of Parliament, in truſt for the State ;—juſt as Wales, or any other county in England. This plain and natural ſtate of the caſe obviates entirely the few captious cavils, with which the Doctor embarraſſes the ſubject. See above, *page* 13.

§ 11. It is a groſs miſrepreſentation of matters, to call the preſent conteſt with the Colonies,—" a conteſt for the *extenſion of dominion and power over* OTHERS, *over* DIFFERENT *ſocieties* ;—*for power only, for its own ſake, abſtracted from all the advantages connected with it* ;—*for reducing our* BRETHREN *to ſervitude* :——to charge it poſitively, *not* to any injury they have done us, but to a *luſt* and *love* of *mere power*, to *pride, blind reſentment, love of revenge, a deſpotic ſpirit, and ſuch curſed ambition as led a* CÆSAR *and an* ALEXANDER, *and many other mad conquerors, to attack*

attack peaceful communities and to lay waste the earth." * I forbear to point out the contradiction the author falls into in this reprefentation, as well as in the general tenor of his pamphlet, by terming the Colonies, fometimes a *different community* and *people* from ourfelves, under a *diftinct government* of *their own*, and then again *our fellow-fubjects* and *brethren*, juft as beft fuits his purpofe : nor fhall I ftop at the unwarrantable partiality, unfairnefs, and abfurdity of the above paffionate language, which contains nothing but flame without light, and muft be generally difapproved.   I fhall content myfelf, with oppofing to his mifreprefentation a juft account of the matter; which is this :—The Colonies deny, according to Doctor PRICE himfelf, " the plenitude of the Parliament's " power over them, and infift on being treated " as free communities ;" † this it is that juftly

draws

---

* See page 51—54, 59, 98, 99, 89.

† See page 56. I have made free, in this paffage, to fubftitute *the Parliament's Power*, inftead of the author's phrafe, *our power* ;—becaufe it is not any power of *this Country* over the Colonies, but that of *Parliament*, that is in conteft : *we* are only interefted as *fellow-fubjects*. The Doctor's phrafeology in this refpect is exceedingly culpable throughout his whole pamphlet, as it fuggefts a very falfe and improper ftate of the cafe.

draws down our refentment upon them: the object of the conteft is therefore, to maintain, not over *others*, but over our *own peop'e*, our own *fellow-citizens*, the fupreme authority of the Legiflature; not to reduce our brethren to fervitude, but to maintain their joint union with us under the fovereign fupremacy of Parliament; and that, not for the fake of *mere power*, *abftracted from all advantages connected with it* (which is a moft wild charge), but for the fake of *public intereft connected with it and dependent on it*.

This is the conteft of the *Parliament* and of the *Nation:*—what improper paffions or motives may actuate fome *individuals*, perhaps Doctor PRICE may know better than we country gentlemen; I am not concerned to inveftigate, much lefs to excufe or defend them.

The Doctor would afk nothing but the *gratitude* and the *commerce* of the Colonies: † the latter is a claim not a little arbitrary on a *free* people, and what, upon his own principles, they would refufe, as a demand of *right*, and could not agree to give up for the next generation; hence alfo Lord SHELBURNE's plan is

G   inconfiltent

* See page 53, 51.   † See page 92.

inconfiftent with the Doctor's theory. As to *gratitude*, we know very little of its fenfe or operations among bodies politic.

He afks——" What have they done? Have " they croffed the ocean and invaded us? " Have they attempted to take from us the " fruits of our labor, and to overturn that " form of government, which we hold fo fa- " cred? This can not be pretended. On the " contrary. This is what we have done to them. " We have tranfported ourfelves to their peace- " ful retreats, and employed our fleets and " armies, to ftop up their ports, to deftroy " their commerce, to feize their effects, and to " burn their towns. Would we but let them " alone, and fuffer them to enjoy in fecurity " their property and governments, inftead of " difturbing us, they would thank and blefs " us. And yet it is we, who imagine our- " felves ill ufed." *

This requires no other anfwer, than to fup- pofe for a moment, that the County of Dur- ham denied the plenitude of Parliamentary power over them, and infifted upon being treated as *a free community* (which the Doctor

allows

* See page 55.

allows to be the avowed pretenfion of the Colonies *), and that the Parliament endeavoured
to reduce them by force to the fame fubordination as the reft of the ftate;—would not the
talking in fuch a ftrain as the above be looked
upon as ftrangely wild and abfurd? It is, at
the beft, a mere begging the queftion, and
fuppofing the Colonies to be diftinct communities
from us, which have governments of their own,
and done us no wrong or injury at all; which
things ought to have been *proved,* agreeable to
the profeffed intent of the Pamphlet.

§ 12. In page 41 and 100, there is a very
fallacious ftate of the reafoning made ufe of by
the advocates of Parliamentary fupremacy.
Doctor PRICE fays,—" that we plead the de-
" fective ftate of the reprefentation of this
" kingdom to prove our right to tax Ameri-
" ca; arguing, that we fubmit to a Parliament
" that does not reprefent us, therefore they
" ought; that we want liberty, and therefore
" they ought." This he calls a *ftrange* argument; and fo indeed it would be. But what
the Doctor alludes to, is not an *argument* to
prove the Parliament's right to tax the Colonies,——but a particular *anfwer* to an *objection*

G 2

made

made by them againſt that right. The caſe is this. The leaders of our fellow-ſubjects in America object,—" that they have no ſhare in making the laws, no voice in Parliament, neither in perſon, nor by repreſentatives of their own chooſing, and are therefore not taxed by themſelves as we are:"—We anſwer; you are in the ſame predicament, in this reſpect, as moſt other individuals and bodies of men in Great Britain are; you have therefore no more right to diſpute the authority of Parliament, on the mere pretext of not being there by a perſonal or delegated preſence, than they have. We mean not hereby to juſtify, much leſs to *prove*, the legal and conſtitutional authority of Parliament over the Colonies; that reſts on other grounds: nor do we hereby aſſert, that they are on an equality with us, in regard to checks upon the abuſe of that authority; we acknowledge, at leaſt I and many more do, that there is a conſiderable difference in this reſpect to their diſadvantage; ſee the preceding 6th §. We only mean to aſſert from plain fact, and the hiſtory of our Conſtitution, that the legal authority of Parliament over perſons and their concerns, for the purpoſes of Government, depends not on their participating in that authority, either in perſon, or by repreſentatives of their own choice;

and

TO A FRIEND.

and that confequently our fellow-fubjects in
America argue badly, when they object,—" we
are not reprefented in Parliament by delegates
of our own choofing; we fhare not in the power
of taxation or legiflation exercifed by Parliament; THEREFORE we are not legally and conftitutionally fubject to Parliamentary taxation
and legiflation."

§ 13. Doctor PRICE fays he hears it conti-
nually urged—" Are they not our fubjects?" *
—I can not remember it having occurred in
my hearing; but it is certainly a falfe plea;
and his reply is a juft one, viz. that they are
not *our fubjects*, but *our fellow-fubjects*: and it is
precifely from this quality, that we conclude
they are jointly fubject with us to the one fupreme and fovereign legiflature of Parliament,
unlefs they can plead any legal exemption by
charter, grant, or compact. How amazingly
does this contradict his reprefentation of the
Colonies, in other places, as *another people* under a *diftinct government of their own!*

§ 14. " The fundamental principle," fays
Doctor PRICE, " of our Government is—*the*
" *right*

* See page 99.

" *right of a people to give and grant their own mo-*
" *ney.*"*

I can not find any such principle. The principles of our Constitution, in regard to taxation, are, 1ft, That no tax can be laid on British subjects without the consent and authority
of Parliament; but that every tax laid on by
that authority is legal and valid: 2dly, That the
House of Commons has the accuftomed right
of apportioning and fixing the fums to be le-
vied on the community for the public fervice,
and of thus giving and granting to the Crown
the neceffary fupplies with the joint affent and
authority of the other two couftituent parts of
the Legiflature, the King and the House of
Lords.——If the House of Commons be confidered as the Reprefentative of the people at
large, then the Doctor's principle may be admitted with fome little qualification thus ; " the
right of the people to give and grant their own
money, *viz.* by certain legal and conftitutional
reprefentatives, eligible according to *cuftom* or
ftatute." The people themfelves *confent* juft as
much and as little to thofe *gifts* and *grants* of
money, as they do to the making of laws, or
any other operation of Parliament; and therefore

* See page 42.

fore " the right of the people to *make laws for themselves*" is juft as much, in the fame fenfe, and in the fame degree, a fundamental princi-ple of our government as " their right to *give and grant their own money.*" The confent of the people has no more conftitutional connection with taxation, than with every other govern-mental power of Parliament: why Doctor PRICE reftrains it more peculiarly to that par-ticular branch.is beft known to himfelf.—There are doubtlefs many *fundamental principles* of our government, that moft prevalently militate againft the principles and arguments of his Pamphlet.

But the Doctor fays;—" this right of a peo-ple to give and grant their own. money, is however the *principle* on which a *free* govern-ment, as fuch, is founded :"*—this is not true according to his theory; for the *principle* of a *free government,* as fuch, agreeable to that theo-ry, is " the right of a people to be *governed* in every refpect by their own will :" fee Sect. 3d of the fubfequent *Obfervations.* Neither was it for any *fuch felf-government* or *felf-taxation* that re-fiftance was made to King CHARLES the firft †; —it was for levying money *without confent of Parliament:*

' See page 49.   † Ibid.

Parlinment.—" Can we with any decency pre-
" tend, that when we give the King *their* mo-
" ney (viz. of the Colonies) we give him *our*
own ?" *. Muft it be repeated again, that WE
give not, nor claim a right to give or grant,
their money to the Crown ? It is the fupreme
Legiflature of the Britifh empire, that claims
the right of impofing taxes on them ; and when
the Commons give the King the money of our
fellow-fubjeéts in America, they juft *as much*
give him *their own,* as when they give him the
money of the people of *Yorkfhire :* in faét, they
give *their own* in neither cafe, but, as was faid
before, they apportion the neceffary fupplies to
be raifed on the community, or if you pleafe
fo to exprefs it,——they *give* the money of *the
Community.*

. I juft defire. tranfitorily to remark,——that
among the caufes of the noble refiftance made
by the *Dutch* to the *Spanifh* monarchy, the Doctor has by miftake mentioned " the levying
" money without their confent :" † for in the
fenfe here intended, the *Dutch* people did not
at that time claim,, nor do at prefent exercife,
any fuch right as Doétor PRICE contends for,
of not being taxed but by their own confent,
                                        either

* See page 50.   † See page 90.

either in perſon, or by repreſentatives of their own chooſing. Taxation *without conſent* of the *Nobles and States of the Provinces*,—was the grievance here alluded to : for the reſt, the caſes of the *Dutch* then, and the American Colonies at preſent, are totally diſſimilar.

§ 15. I flatter myſelf Doctor PRICE will do me the juſtice to rank me among thoſe *ſome,* who he doubts not " are influenced by no other " principle, than a regard to what they think " the juſt authority of Parliament over the Co- " lonies *, and to the unity and indiviſibility of " the Britiſh empire. I wiſh," ſays he, " ſuch " could be engaged to enter thoroughly into " the enquiry, which has been the ſubject of " the firſt part of this pamphlet, and to conſi- " der, particularly, how different a thing main- " taining the authority of government *within* a " ſtate is from maintaining the authority of one " people over another, already happy in the " enjoyment of a government of their own." †
—I have examined thoroughly the firſt part of the Doctor's pamphlet, witneſs the *Obſervations*

H   hereto

* I have here again ſubſtituted the *Parliament* inſtead of *this country,* for the reaſon alledged above, page 48, in the *Note.*

† See page 56.

hereto annexed; the refult will there be feen: for the reft, what follows is not at all applicable here; for we deem not the Colonies by any means *another people*, under diftinƈt fupreme free *governments of their own*, but a people *within the ftate*, juft as the people of Yorkfhire are: but it is one of Doƈtor PRICE's favorite and capital mifreprefentations, to talk of them throughout his whole piece in the former ftrain, which is nothing but a moft exceptionable taking for granted the very thing in difpute;— an eafy method indeed, that fpares the trouble of arguing! As well might you talk of *Briftol* or *York* being a different people,—and argue that they have governments of their own, which the Parliament ought not to interfere in: they are indeed different as to place or other particular circumftances, but they are the *fame people* or *civil community*, and though endowed with diftinƈt fubordinate Legiflatures for particular purpofes, yet are united in the fame bonds under one and the fame fupreme legiflative authority. I refer you, for confirmation of this, to the preceding part of this letter. Moft of the Doƈtor's reafonings in favor of the American Colonies, throughout his pamphlet, derive a confiderable degree of their plaufibility from that affumed hypothefis juft now cenfured,—and

alfo

also from stating the contest to be betwixt *this kingdom* and those *foreign* states, the Colonies, as if *we* here in this island claimed jurisdiction, or desired to extend dominion over *them:* we only claim to be their *fellow-subjects.* See *note,* § 11. *

The Doctor wishes us further to consider,——
" that the desire of maintaining authority is
" only warrantable, as far as it is the means
" of promoting some end and doing some
" good;" (this every body is agreed in) " and
" that, before we resolve to spread famine and
" fire through a country, in order to make it
" acknowledge our authority, we ought to be
" assured, that great advantages will arise not
" only to ourselves, but to the country we wish
" to conquer." †. Always misrepresentation!
We do not want to make the Colonies acknowledge *our* authority, but that of the *supreme Legislature,* and *our joint civil union* and *submission* under that authority. The great advantages proposed are the continuance and security of those benefits we have already experienced, or may further derive from that mutual union and

H 2 connection.

_____

* See PRICE's *Observations,* &c. page 19, 20, 27, 28, 32, 35, 36, 51, 53, 56, &c. &c. throughout.

† See page 56, 57.

connection. But the doctrine of *assurance* is as little necessary to action in worldly concerns as in religion : if nations and communities were never to go to war or vindicate their rights, but when *assured* of the great advantages to be derived from so doing,—ambition and injustice would speedily divest them of their most valuable rights and property. But this is too evident to require any further illustration.

Having now, Sir! as I presume, sufficiently explained to you my sentiments on the subject you desired, and also the principles on which they rest, and by which the main force of Doctor Price's reasonings may be easily obviated, I therefore make an end of this epistle, with the assurance of my being

Yours, &c.

H. GOODRICKE.

York,
May 1, 1776.

www.ingramcontent.com/pod-product-compliance
Lightning Source LLC
Chambersburg PA
CBHW021627270326
41931CB00008B/898